CGP

Fractions Activity Book

for ages 7-8

This CGP book is bursting with fun activities
to build up children's skills and confidence.

It's ideal for extra practice to reinforce what
they're learning in primary school. Enjoy!

Published by CGP

Editors:
Michael Bushell, Liam Dyer, Sean McParland and Ben Train

Proofreaders:
Gail Renaud and Glenn Rogers

With thanks to Emily Smith for the copyright research.

ISBN: 978 1 78908 711 6

Graphics used on the cover and throughout the book © www.edu-clips.com
Cover design concept by emc design ltd.

Printed by Elanders Ltd, Newcastle upon Tyne.

Contents

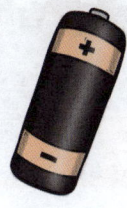

Fractions of Shapes   2

Tenths   4

Fractions of Objects   6

Equivalent Fractions   8

Adding Fractions   10

Subtracting Fractions   12

Puzzle: High Street Jumble   14

Ordering Fractions 1   16

Ordering Fractions 2   18

On the Number Line   20

Fractions of Amounts 1   22

Fractions of Amounts 2   24

Fraction Problems   26

Answers   28

Fractions of Shapes

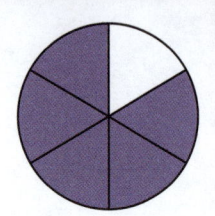
 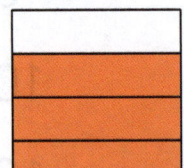 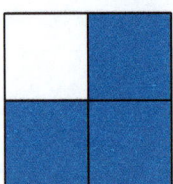  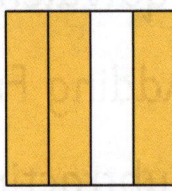 
Now Try These

1. Fill in the boxes to complete the fractions below.

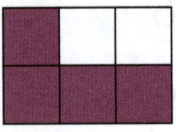 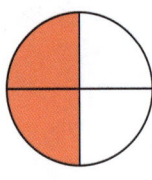 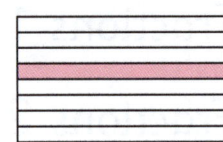 

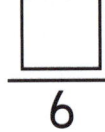
$\frac{\Box}{6}$

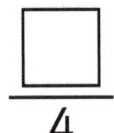
$\frac{\Box}{4}$

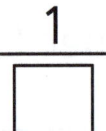
$\frac{1}{\Box}$

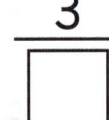
$\frac{3}{\Box}$

2. Colour in the shapes to show each fraction.

 $\frac{1}{3}$ 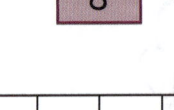 $\frac{5}{8}$ $\frac{1}{2}$ $\frac{3}{5}$

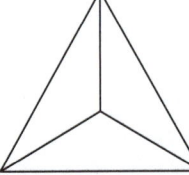 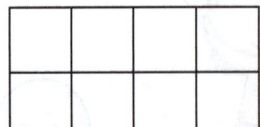  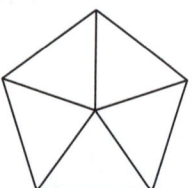

3. Draw lines to match up the shapes that have the same fraction shaded.
   Write the fraction next to each line you draw.

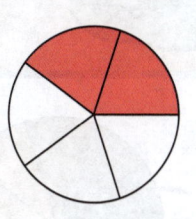
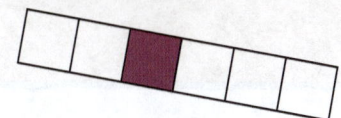
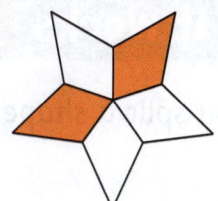
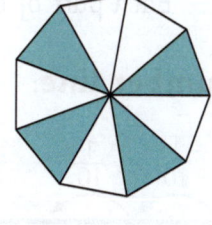

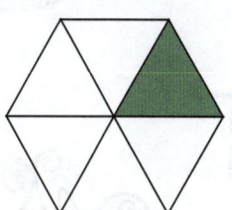

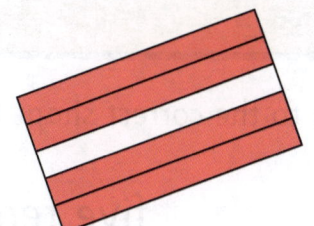
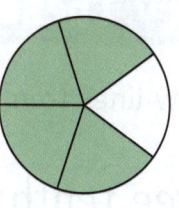

An Extra Challenge

Look at the blocks each runner is standing on below.

a) Which block is half the size of 3rd?

b) Which block is $\frac{1}{5}$ the size of 1st?

c) Choose fractions from the box below to complete these sentences.

   (i) 3rd is .... the size of 2nd.

   (ii) 2nd is .... the size of 1st.

$\frac{1}{3}$	$\frac{2}{3}$	$\frac{2}{5}$	$\frac{3}{5}$	$\frac{4}{5}$

Are your fractions skills shaping up nicely?

3

Tenths

How It Works

If you split a shape into **ten equal parts**, you get **tenths**.

Each part of the circle is $\frac{1}{10}$: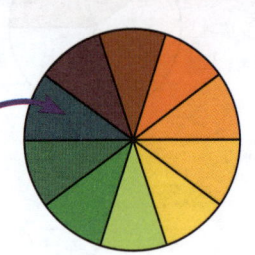

You can also count up in **tenths** on a **number line**:

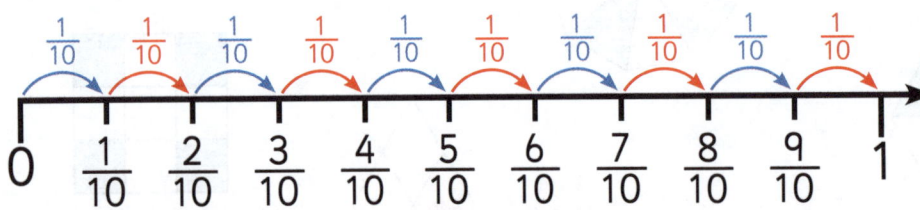

Now Try These

1. Draw lines to match each fraction to the correct shape below.

three tenths $\frac{4}{10}$ five tenths $\frac{7}{10}$

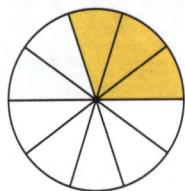  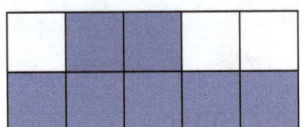 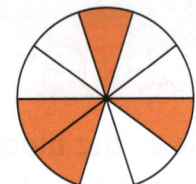

2. The diagram below shows the roof panels of a big tent.

a) What fraction of the roof panels are grey?

b) What fraction of the roof panels are red?

4

3. Complete the sentences using the signs below. You won't need to use all the signs.

a) Start at $\frac{5}{10}$ and count up three tenths — you get ☐

b) One tenth more than $\frac{1}{10}$ is ☐

c) $\frac{4}{10}$ is two tenths ☐ than $\frac{2}{10}$

d) Start at $\frac{9}{10}$ and count down ☐ tenths — you get $\frac{2}{10}$

An Extra Challenge

Beebe writes down her tent number in a secret code.
She leaves clues hidden in the shapes below.

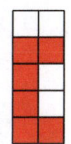 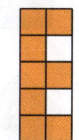  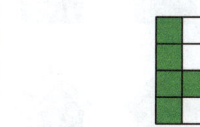  

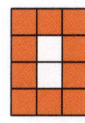   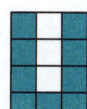 

Find the shape above that matches each fraction, and write down the letter hidden inside to reveal Beebe's tent number.

$\frac{7}{10}$ $\frac{5}{10}$ $\frac{9}{10}$ $\frac{8}{10}$

....

Hope that wasn't too in-tenths.
I mean in-tents. No, intense...

 ☐   ☐    ☐

5

Fractions of Objects

You can **find fractions** of sets of objects by **sharing** them into **equal groups**.

If you share a set of objects into **3** equal groups, then each group is $\frac{1}{3}$. For example:

Draw rings to share **6 sticks** into **3 equal groups**, and use these to find $\frac{2}{3}$ of 6.

1 group is $\frac{1}{3}$, so 2 groups are $\frac{2}{3}$. There are 4 sticks in 2 groups. So $\frac{2}{3}$ of 6 = 4.

Now Try These

1. Draw rings around these sets to share equally into:

   a) 2 groups.

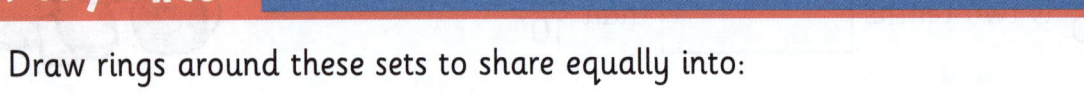

$\frac{1}{2}$ of 10 = ...

   b) 4 groups.

$\frac{1}{4}$ of 16 = ...

2. Fill in the box to show what fraction of these tennis balls are blue.

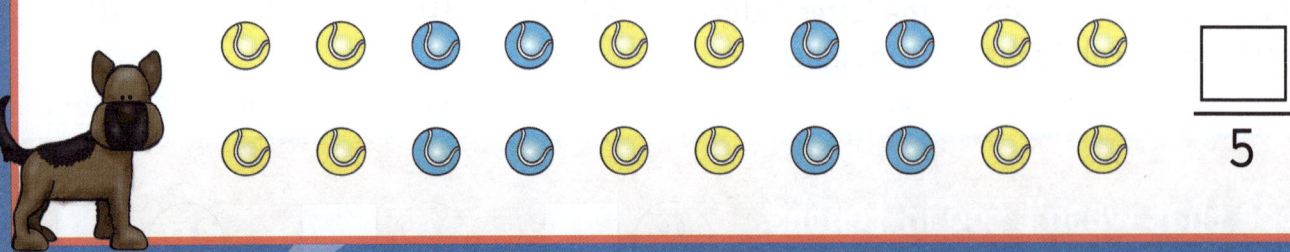

$\dfrac{\boxed{}}{5}$

3. Maya has finished her homework... but her dog has eaten part of it!
   Look at Maya's working out and write the missing numbers in the boxes.

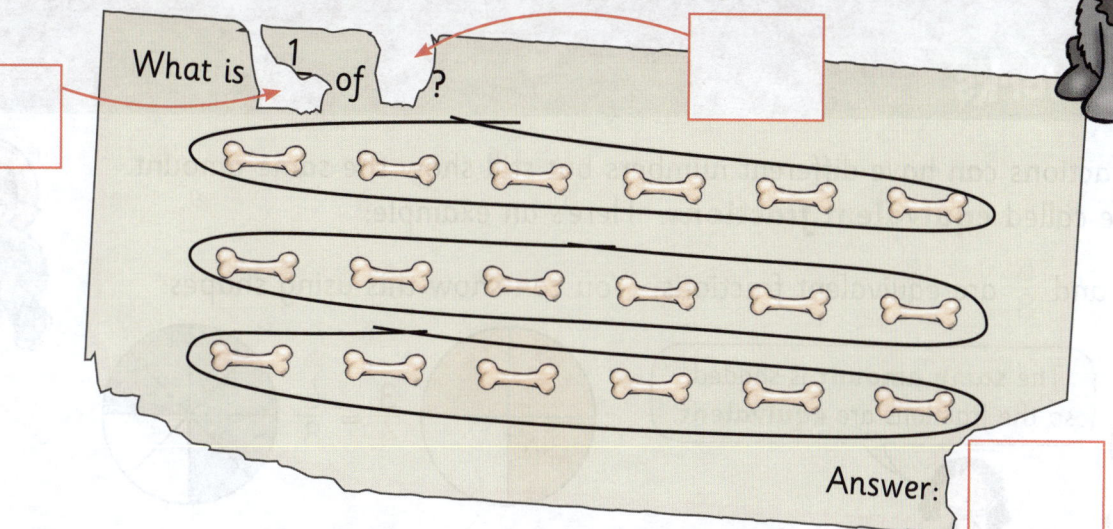

What is $\frac{1}{\boxed{}}$ of $\boxed{}$?

Answer: $\boxed{}$

4. Ana and Leo both take a fraction of their dog biscuits.

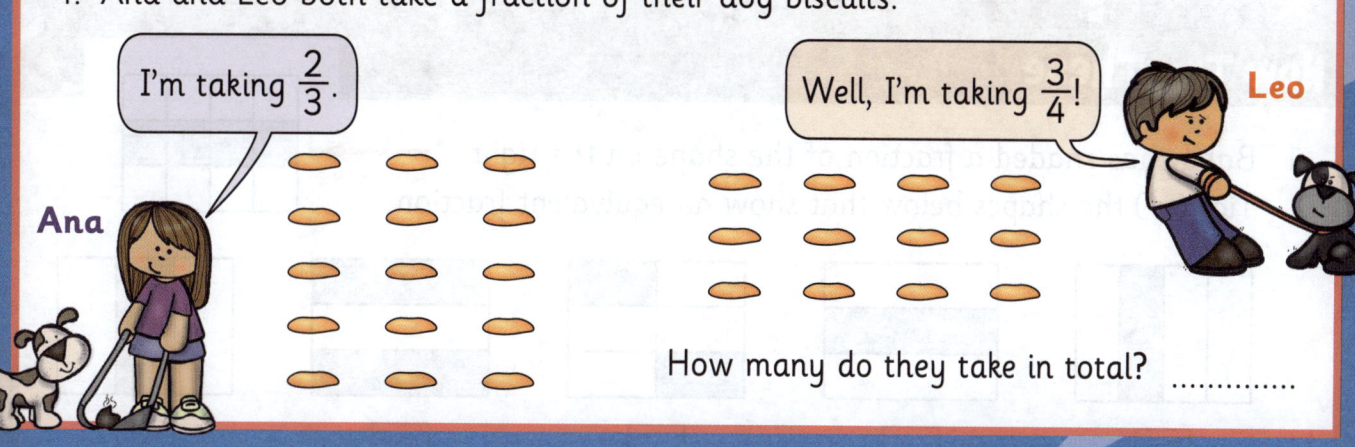

Ana: I'm taking $\frac{2}{3}$.

Leo: Well, I'm taking $\frac{3}{4}$!

How many do they take in total? ....

An Extra Challenge

Brian sees two groups of dogs at a park.

These dogs are **grey**.

These dogs are **brown**.

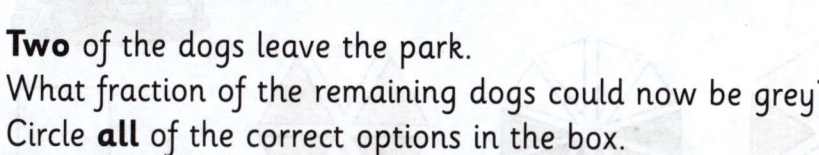
Two of the dogs leave the park.
What fraction of the remaining dogs could now be grey?
Circle **all** of the correct options in the box.

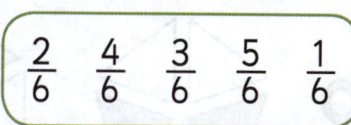
$\frac{2}{6}$ $\frac{4}{6}$ $\frac{3}{6}$ $\frac{5}{6}$ $\frac{1}{6}$

Do you want to share how
well you did on this topic?

7

Equivalent Fractions

How It Works

Two fractions can have different numbers but still show the same amount. They're called **equivalent fractions**. Here's an example:

$\frac{3}{4}$ and $\frac{6}{8}$ are equivalent fractions. You can show this using shapes:

The **same amount** is shaded, so the fractions are **equivalent**.

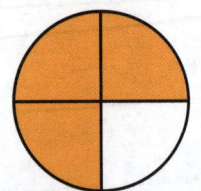 $\frac{3}{4} = \frac{6}{8}$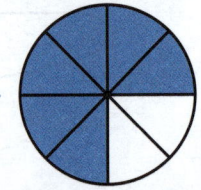

Now Try These

1. Babar has shaded a fraction of the shape on the right. Tick (✔) the shapes below that show an equivalent fraction.

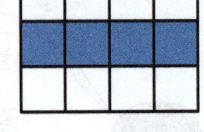

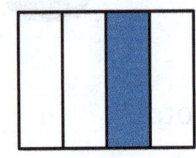 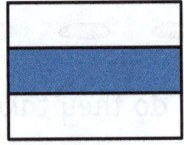 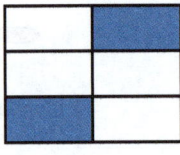 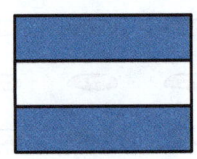 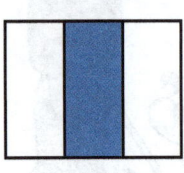

2. Shade the shapes and fill in the boxes to complete these equivalent fractions.

a) 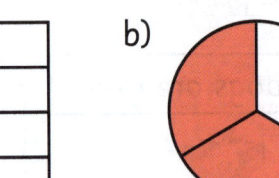 $\frac{1}{2} = \frac{\square}{4}$

b) 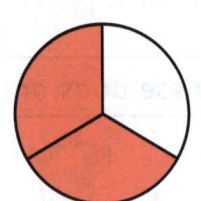 $\frac{2}{3} = \frac{\square}{6}$

3. Circle the set of shapes below that shows an equivalent fraction to $\frac{3}{5}$. Write down the fraction that you've circled.

$\frac{3}{5} = \frac{\square}{\square}$

4. Draw lines to match equivalent fractions using the shaded shapes in the middle. One has been done for you.

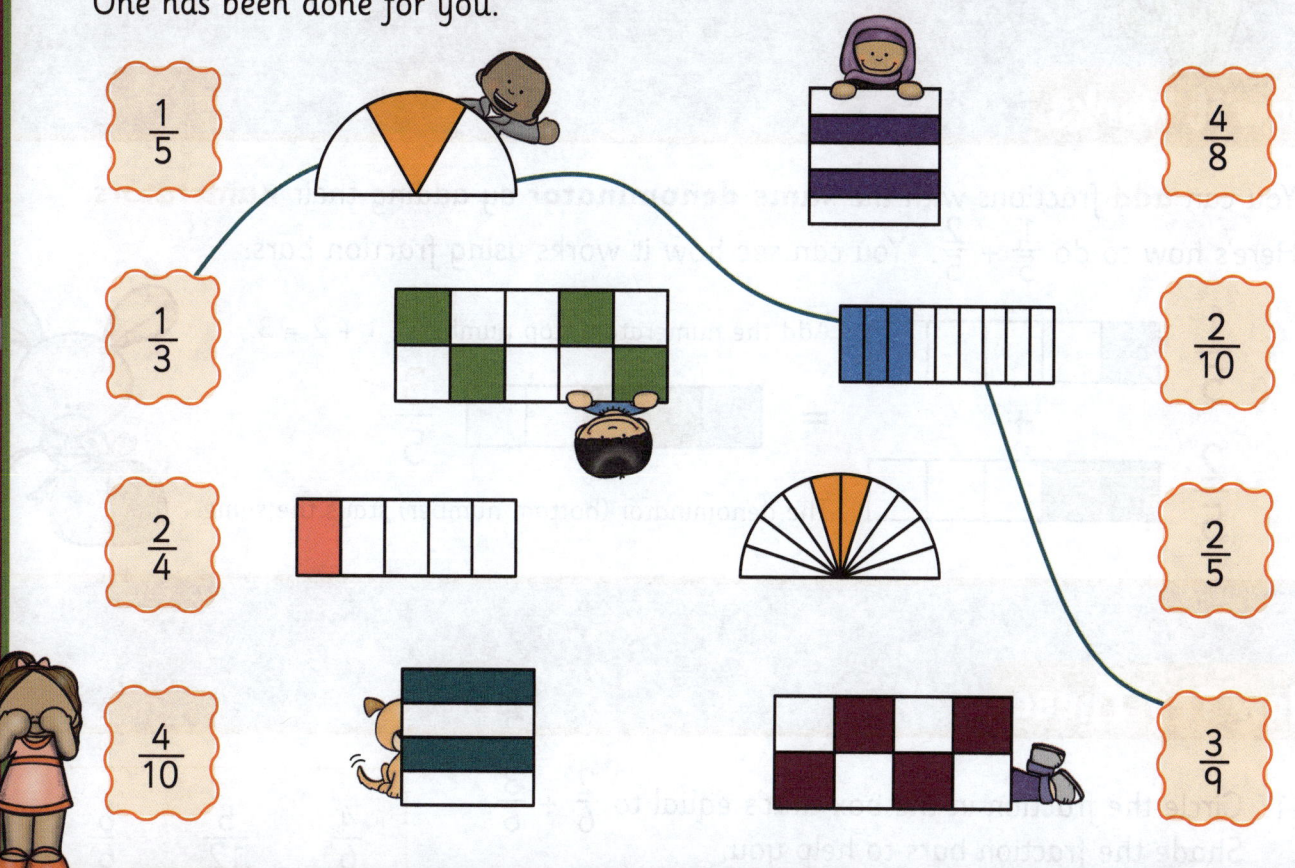

$\frac{1}{5}$

$\frac{1}{3}$

$\frac{2}{4}$

$\frac{4}{10}$

$\frac{4}{8}$

$\frac{2}{10}$

$\frac{2}{5}$

$\frac{3}{9}$

An Extra Challenge

An animal has been playing on this hopscotch court!

a) What fraction of the squares on the court are covered by paw prints?

b) The animal that left the prints is shown below an equivalent fraction to the fraction in part a). Circle the correct animal.

$\frac{3}{5}$ $\frac{6}{10}$ $\frac{3}{6}$ $\frac{4}{12}$ $\frac{1}{4}$

Tick the equivalent box to how you feel about fractions!

Adding Fractions

How It Works

You can **add** fractions with the **same denominator** by adding their **numerators**.
Here's how to do $\frac{1}{5} + \frac{2}{5}$. You can see how it works using fraction bars:

$\frac{1}{5}$

$+$

$\frac{2}{5}$

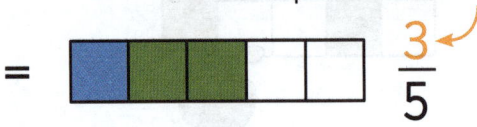

Add the numerators (top numbers): 1 + 2 = 3.

$\frac{3}{5}$

The denominator (bottom number) stays the same.

Now Try These

1. Circle the fraction in the box that's equal to $\frac{2}{6} + \frac{3}{6}$.
   Shade the fraction bars to help you.

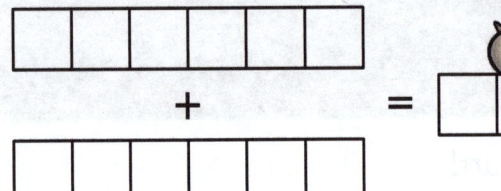

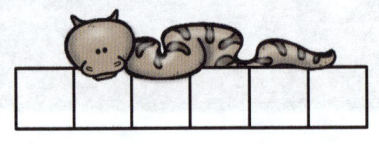

$\frac{4}{6}$	$\frac{5}{12}$	$\frac{6}{6}$
	$\frac{5}{6}$	$\frac{6}{12}$
$\frac{6}{5}$	$\frac{2}{3}$	$\frac{3}{5}$

2. Fill in the boxes and shade the shapes to complete these fraction sums.

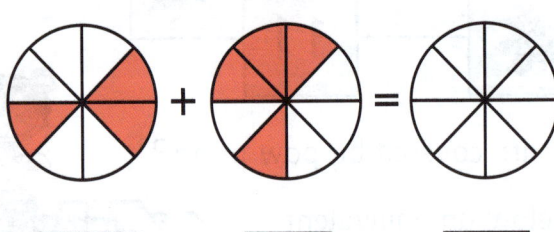

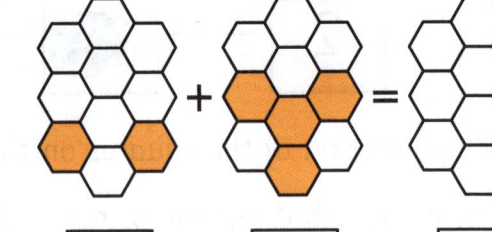

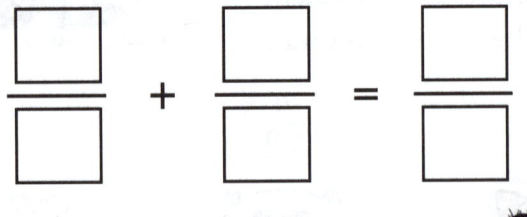

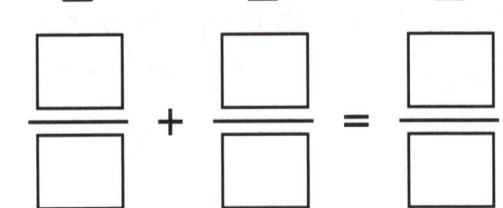

3. Work out:

   a) $\frac{4}{7} + \frac{1}{7} =$ ....

   b) $\frac{5}{13} + \frac{5}{13} =$ ....

10

4. Draw lines to match each fraction to the correct sum.

 $\frac{9}{12}$  $\frac{6}{9}$  $\frac{6}{12}$  $\frac{8}{12}$  $\frac{8}{9}$

$\frac{4}{12} + \frac{5}{12}$ $\frac{3}{9} + \frac{3}{9}$

$\frac{2}{12} + \frac{6}{12}$ $\frac{3}{9} + \frac{5}{9}$  $\frac{5}{12} + \frac{1}{12}$

5. Two camels are drinking water.

  a) Sandy drinks $\frac{3}{11}$ of the water and Lippy drinks $\frac{2}{11}$ of the water.

  What fraction of the water did they drink altogether?

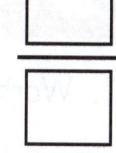

  b) Sandy drinks another $\frac{6}{11}$ of the water.

  What fraction of the water did Sandy drink in total?

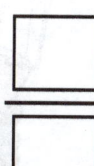

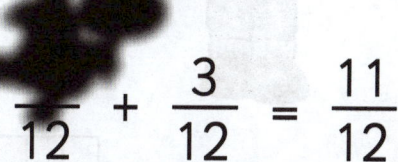

An Extra Challenge

These animals are covering some numbers with their shadows.
Work out the numbers that are in the shade.

$\frac{2}{5} + \frac{}{5} = \frac{4}{5}$ $\frac{5}{8} + \frac{}{8} = \frac{8}{8}$ $\frac{}{12} + \frac{3}{12} = \frac{11}{12}$

How are you with fraction
sums? Add a tick to a box!

Subtracting Fractions

How It Works

To **subtract** fractions with the **same denominator**, just subtract their **numerators**. You can use a diagram to check your answer — here's how:

What is $\frac{5}{6} - \frac{3}{6}$?   Subtract the numerators: $5 - 3 = 2$ So $\frac{5}{6} - \frac{3}{6} = \frac{2}{6}$

$$\frac{5}{6} \qquad - \qquad \frac{3}{6} \qquad = \qquad \frac{2}{6}$$

Now Try These

1. Work out these subtraction problems.

$\frac{4}{5} - \frac{1}{5}$

−

=

$\frac{3}{6} - \frac{2}{6}$

−

=
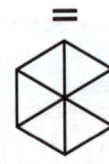

$\frac{6}{9} - \frac{2}{9}$

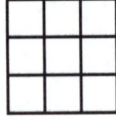
−
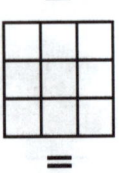
=
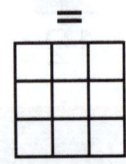

$\frac{8}{9} - \frac{6}{9}$

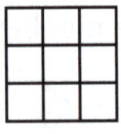
−
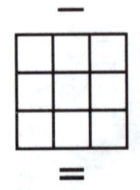
=

2. Eric has $\frac{5}{8}$ of a book left to read. He reads another $\frac{2}{8}$.

   What fraction of the book does he have left to read now?

   ....

3. Write the numbers 5, 6, 8 and 9 in the boxes to make these subtractions correct.

$$\frac{11}{12} - \frac{\boxed{}}{12} = \frac{5}{12} \qquad \frac{\boxed{}}{12} - \frac{7}{12} = \frac{2}{12} \qquad \frac{\boxed{}}{12} - \frac{\boxed{}}{12} = \frac{3}{12}$$

4. Sumati removes $\frac{3}{10}$ of the books from a bookshelf.

   What fraction of the books are left on the bookshelf?

....

An Extra Challenge

| Joanna thinks of a fraction and whispers it to Oli. | Oli subtracts a fraction and whispers the answer to Caleb. | Caleb subtracts another fraction, then whispers the answer to Isabella. |

$\frac{10}{11}$

$\frac{4}{11}$

Isabella is thinking of the final answer.

Find a pair of fractions that Oli and Caleb could have subtracted.
How many other pairs can you find?

How much did you take away from these pages?

High Street Jumble

Tess is doing some shopping around town. She picks up a letter from each shop.

Unscramble the letters at the end to help Tess answer Leah's question.

HIGH STREET

Flora's Floral Florist

Draw straight lines to connect the dots next to pairs of flowers that show the same amount.

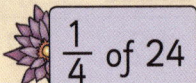 $\frac{1}{3}$ of 15 •

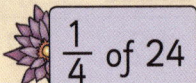 $\frac{1}{5}$ of 35 •

$\frac{1}{4}$ of 24 •

E
D
I
M

 • 7

• 6

• 5

Tess keeps the only letter that isn't crossed out.

Beth & Belinda's Bakery

Tess buys herself a treat at the bakery. The thing she buys is on the same spot on the number line as the answer to $\frac{11}{12} - \frac{4}{12}$.

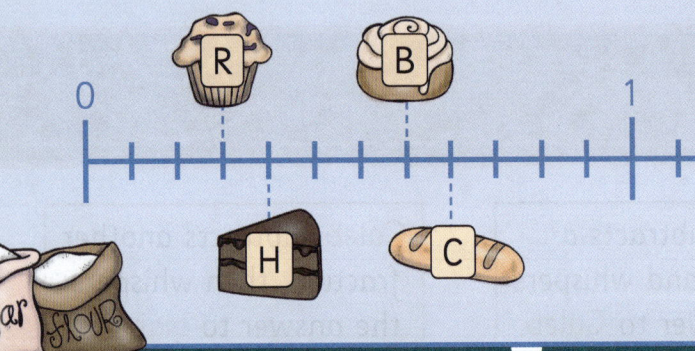

R   B   F

0   1

H   C

Bijoya's Boutique

Tess tries on a few tops at the boutique.

 18 — N

 O — 6

 14 — A

 W — 12

 5 — C

She buys the top with the number that's 2 more than $\frac{3}{5}$ of 20.

14

Gofraid's Grocers

Here are some of the things she buys at the grocer's:

 N $\frac{5}{8}$  L $\frac{1}{8}$  G $\frac{8}{5}$  F $\frac{6}{8}$  T $\frac{5}{16}$

She writes down the letter on the item that shows the answer to $\frac{2}{8} + \frac{3}{8}$.

Nick's Newsagents

Tess sees some newspaper headlines that mention fractions.

Only $\frac{1}{7}$ of towns have a town mascot

Snow covers $\frac{1}{9}$ of town

Unlucky $\frac{1}{13}$ of bakers drop flour

Roughly $\frac{1}{10}$ of hedges don't have hedgehogs

Crowd only watches $\frac{1}{18}$ of match

She finds the second largest fraction, then writes down the first letter of that headline.

Keep track of her letters here:

Florist	Grocers	Newsagents	Bakery	Boutique

Did you get everything that you needed?

I think so... wait, I forgot the .... !

Ordering Fractions 1

How It Works

When you're comparing fractions, take a look at the **denominators**.
If they're the **same**, then use the **numerators** to decide which fraction is bigger:

$\frac{3}{4}$ $\frac{1}{4}$ These two fractions have the same denominator...
...so compare the numerators.

3 is **bigger** than 1, so $\frac{3}{4}$ is **bigger** than $\frac{1}{4}$. You can also write this as $\frac{3}{4} > \frac{1}{4}$.

Now Try These

1. Circle the rocket that shows the bigger fraction in each pair.

a)

b)

2. Draw lines to join up each pair of fractions in a correct number sentence.
   One has been done for you.

$\frac{2}{3}$ >   <   = $\frac{1}{3}$ $\frac{2}{6}$ >   <   = $\frac{5}{6}$

$\frac{3}{10}$ >   <   = $\frac{3}{10}$ $\frac{7}{8}$ >   <   = $\frac{1}{8}$

16

3. On a mission to Mars, Neil collects $\frac{2}{12}$ of the rocks, Helen collects $\frac{6}{12}$ and Nyesha collects $\frac{4}{12}$. Who collects the most rocks?

....

4. Write these fractions in order from smallest to largest.

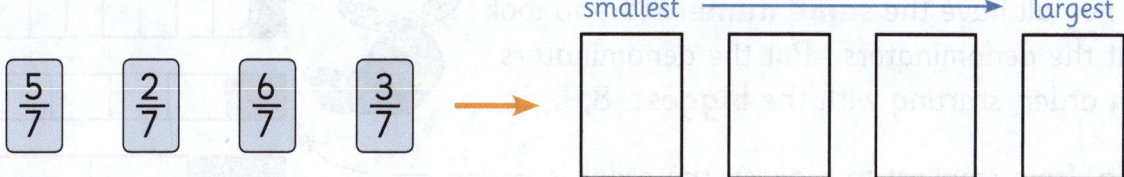

smallest ⟶ largest

$\frac{5}{7}$ $\frac{2}{7}$ $\frac{6}{7}$ $\frac{3}{7}$

5. Three Martians each try out a car and rate it out of 9. Write their names in the order of who liked the car the most.

Ebop   **Sram**   **Val**

$\frac{3}{9}$ $\frac{1}{9}$ $\frac{5}{9}$

most ....

....

least ....

An Extra Challenge

Astronauts earn points for doing tasks on a space station.
On each task, they're put in order by who does the biggest fraction of the work.

Cooking

Mae $\frac{3}{11}$ Peter $\frac{1}{11}$

Matt $\frac{5}{11}$ Lizzy $\frac{2}{11}$

Cleaning

Mae $\frac{3}{14}$ Peter $\frac{4}{14}$

Matt $\frac{1}{14}$ Lizzy $\frac{6}{14}$

They earn 4 points for coming in first, 3 points for second, 2 points for third and 1 point for last.

How many points does each astronaut have?

Was that all alien to you or are you ready for another mission?

Ordering Fractions 2

How It Works

If you're ordering fractions with the same numerator, then you only need to compare their **denominators**. The **bigger** the denominator, the **smaller** the fraction.

For example, here's how you'd put $\frac{1}{5}$, $\frac{1}{3}$ and $\frac{1}{8}$ in order from smallest to biggest:

They all have the **same numerator**, so look at the denominators. Put the denominators in order, starting with the **biggest**: 8, 5, 3.

So, from smallest to biggest, the order is $\frac{1}{8}$, $\frac{1}{5}$, $\frac{1}{3}$.

$\frac{1}{8}$

$\frac{1}{5}$

$\frac{1}{3}$

Now Try These

1. Fill in the gaps with **>** or **<** to make each number sentence correct.

$\frac{1}{2}$ .... $\frac{1}{3}$ $\frac{1}{7}$ .... $\frac{1}{5}$ $\frac{1}{10}$ .... $\frac{1}{4}$

2. These friends are going on a road trip across Canada. In each pair, whoever says the larger fraction goes in Anne's car and the other goes in Tony's.

Maisie   Jos

$\frac{1}{3}$ $\frac{1}{6}$

Lily   Keaton

$\frac{1}{5}$ $\frac{1}{4}$

Benoit   Liu

$\frac{1}{8}$ $\frac{1}{7}$

Write the names next to the correct car.

Anne's car

Tony's car

3. Draw lines to match each fraction to its place when the fractions are put in order from smallest to largest.

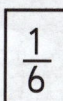 $\frac{1}{6}$ $\frac{1}{8}$ $\frac{1}{12}$

 1st  2nd  3rd  4th  5th  6th

 $\frac{1}{9}$ $\frac{1}{5}$ $\frac{1}{10}$

4. Anne keeps track of the colour of each lighthouse she sees on the road trip. $\frac{1}{7}$ of them are blue, $\frac{1}{6}$ are red, $\frac{1}{11}$ are orange and $\frac{1}{4}$ are white.

Write the colours in order, starting with the one that Anne sees most.

....

most   least

An Extra Challenge

Jos $\frac{1}{7}$

Maisie $\frac{1}{\text{🍁}}$

Tony $\frac{1}{2}$

Liu $\frac{1}{28}$

Lily $\frac{1}{4}$

Five of the friends make some maple syrup.
The tree shows what fraction of the syrup they each made.

Only one person made less syrup than Maisie.
Which leaf shows the denominator of Maisie's fraction?

 5

 14

 29

 30

 3

Nice trip, eh? Could you order fractions from coast to coast?

19

On the Number Line

How It Works

You can show fractions on a number line — here's an example:

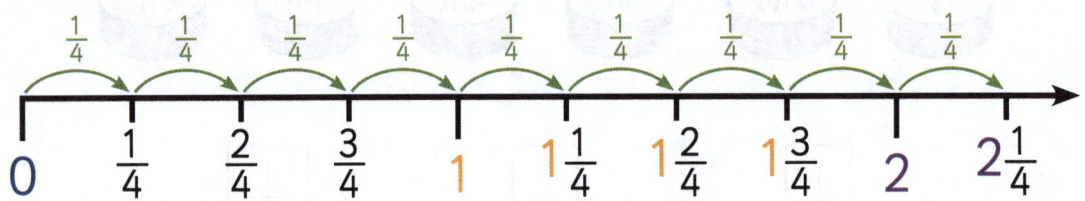

$$\frac{1}{4} \quad \frac{1}{4} \quad \frac{1}{4} \quad \frac{1}{4} \quad \frac{1}{4} \quad \frac{1}{4} \quad \frac{1}{4} \quad \frac{1}{4} \quad \frac{1}{4}$$

$$0 \quad \frac{1}{4} \quad \frac{2}{4} \quad \frac{3}{4} \quad 1 \quad 1\frac{1}{4} \quad 1\frac{2}{4} \quad 1\frac{3}{4} \quad 2 \quad 2\frac{1}{4}$$

There are **4 equal gaps** between each whole number, so you can count in **quarters**.

Now Try These

1. Fill in each box on this number line with the correct fraction.

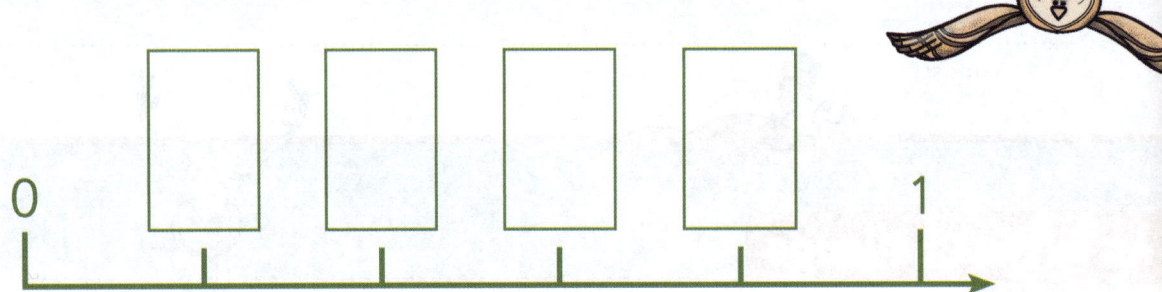

0   1

2. Draw lines to match each fraction to the owl who is perched on its spot on the number line.

$$\frac{1}{3} \qquad \frac{1}{8} \qquad \frac{2}{3} \qquad \frac{1}{4}$$

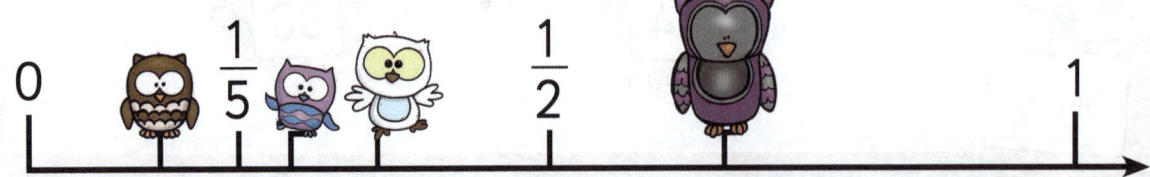

0        $\frac{1}{5}$ $\frac{1}{2}$ 1

3. Fill in the boxes to complete these equivalent fractions.
   Use the number lines to help you.

a)
$$\frac{2}{6} = \frac{\boxed{}}{3}$$

b)
$$\frac{8}{10} = \frac{\boxed{}}{5}$$

4. Colour in the owl on the number that you say as "one and three tenths".

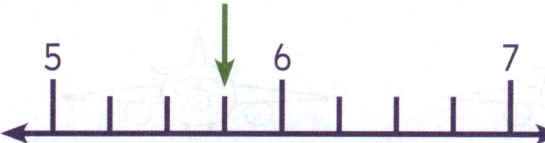

5. What number is the arrow below pointing to?

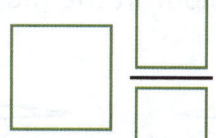

An Extra Challenge

These owls are having some trouble finding their place on the number line.

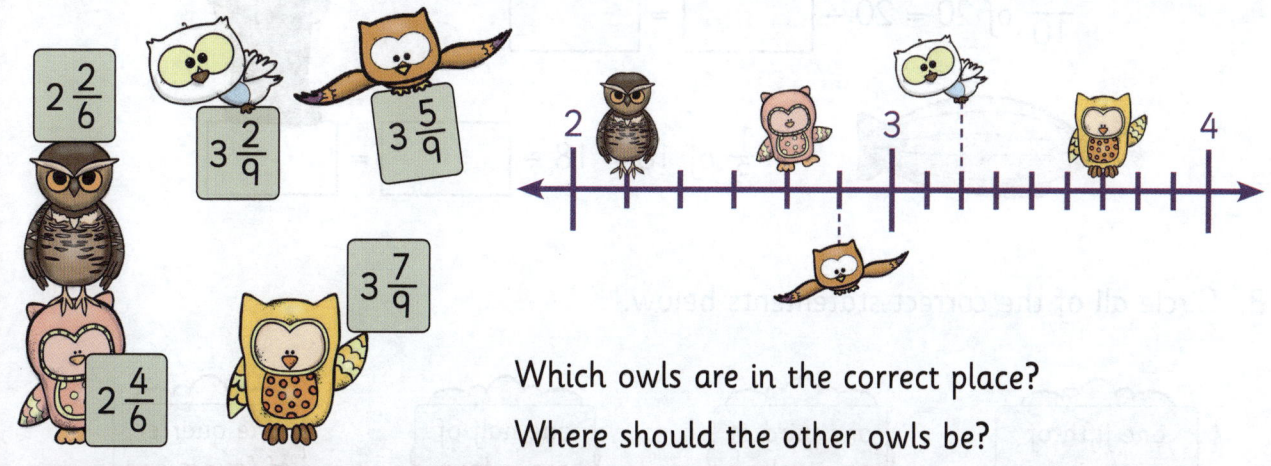

$2\frac{2}{6}$ $3\frac{2}{9}$ $3\frac{5}{9}$ $3\frac{7}{9}$ $2\frac{4}{6}$

Which owls are in the correct place?

Where should the other owls be?

Fractions of Amounts 1

How It Works

You can find a fraction of a **number** or a **measure**.
It is easiest when the fraction has a **1 on top**:

What is $\frac{1}{4}$ of **8**?   Just use division — **divide** by the **bottom number**.
So $\frac{1}{4}$ of 8 = 8 ÷ **4** = **2**.

Or draw **8 objects** and split them into groups.   Split into **4 equal groups**.
Each group has **2 stars**.

So $\frac{1}{4}$ of 8 = **2**.

Now Try These

1. What is $\frac{1}{5}$ of 5? Colour in the planes below to show your answer.

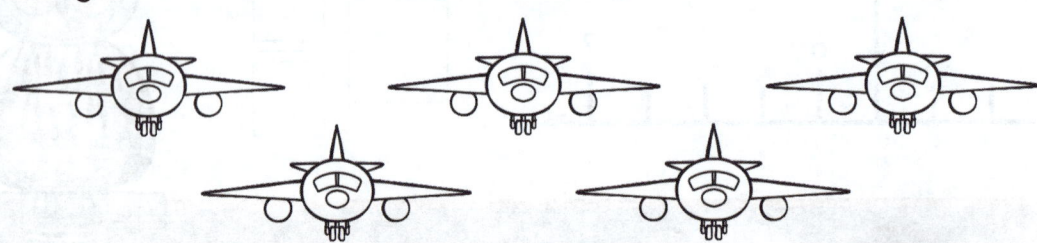

2. Complete these number sentences.

$\frac{1}{10}$ of 20 = 20 ÷ ☐ = ☐

 $\frac{1}{3}$ of 18 = 18 ÷ ☐ = ☐

3. Circle all of the correct statements below.

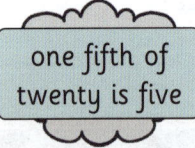 one fifth of twenty is five

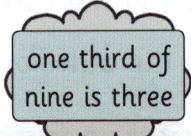 one third of nine is three

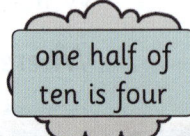 one half of ten is four

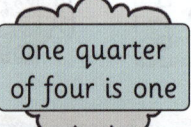 one quarter of four is one

4. Cole sees 32 hot air balloons.

   $\frac{1}{8}$ of them are stripy. How many hot air balloons are stripy?

   .... hot air balloons

5. Draw lines to match each sentence to its missing fraction.

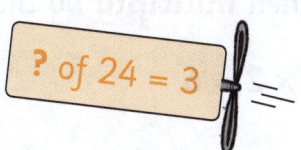
? of 24 = 3

? of 24 = 4

? of 24 = 6

$\frac{1}{4}$

$\frac{1}{8}$

$\frac{1}{6}$

6. These toy helicopters make up $\frac{1}{10}$ of Akio's collection.

   How many helicopters does he have in total?

   .... helicopters

An Extra Challenge

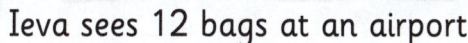

Ieva sees 12 bags at an airport.

   $\frac{1}{4}$ of the bags are black.

   Of those that aren't black, $\frac{1}{9}$ are red.

   Of those that aren't black or red, $\frac{1}{2}$ are brown.

How many bags are brown? Colour in the bags to help you!

   ....

Is your mood sky-high
after these problems?

Fractions of Amounts 2

How It Works

Here's what to do if the fraction has a number **bigger than 1** on the top.

What is $\frac{2}{3}$ of 9?   First **divide** by the bottom, and then **multiply** by the top:

$$\frac{1}{3} \text{ of } 9 = 9 \div 3 = 3. \quad \frac{2}{3} \text{ of } 9 = 3 \times 2 = 6.$$

Or draw **9 objects** and split them into groups.

Split into **3 equal groups**.
Each group has **3 phones**.

One group is $\frac{1}{3}$ of 9 = **3**.

Two groups is $\frac{2}{3}$ of 9 = **6**.

Now Try These

1. Split the computer keys into equal groups to help you work out:

a)

b)

$\frac{1}{4}$ of 8 = ..., $\frac{3}{4}$ of 8 = ... $\frac{1}{5}$ of 10 = ..., $\frac{3}{5}$ of 10 = ...

2. Fill in the boxes to complete these number sentences.

$\frac{1}{3}$ of 6 = ☐ , so $\frac{2}{3}$ of 6 = ☐ × 2 = ☐

$\frac{1}{4}$ of 20 = ☐ , so $\frac{3}{4}$ of 20 = ☐ × 3 = ☐

$\frac{1}{8}$ of 16 = ☐ , so $\frac{5}{8}$ of 16 = ☐ × 5 = ☐

3. Fill in the missing numbers.

My number is **15**.

one fifth is ... `3`   two fifths is ... ☐   three fifths is ... ☐

My number is **30**.

one fifth is ... ☐   three fifths is ... ☐   four fifths is ... ☐

4. Musa has £40. He spends seven tenths of his money on a video game.
   How much did the video game cost?

£ ....

5. Saul records 48 minutes of video.
   $\frac{5}{8}$ of the video is used in a TV show.

   How many minutes of video are used in the TV show?

.... minutes

An Extra Challenge

Alfie is watching the news.
Here are the latest headlines:

£80 raised by Elmrose Primary School.
Three quarters is given to charity!

It's baa-d news for Brimble Farm...
two thirds of their 60 sheep have escaped!

Moon City lose their eighth game — that's
two quarters of the games they've played!

Work out the answers to these problems:

a) How much did Elmrose Primary School give to charity?

b) How many sheep escaped from Brimble Farm?

c) How many games have Moon City played?

Did you get a good amount of
these fraction problems right?

25

Fraction Problems

How It Works

You'll need all your fraction skills to get through these problems. Here's an example:

Find the missing fraction: $\frac{1}{4}$ of 12 = ☐ of 6

$\frac{1}{4}$ of 12 = 12 ÷ 4 = **3**.

You **divide 6 by 2** to get **3**, so $\frac{1}{4}$ of 12 = $\frac{1}{2}$ of 6.

Dividing by 2 is the same as halving.

Now Try These

1. Write the correct fraction in the boxes to show the length of each insect.

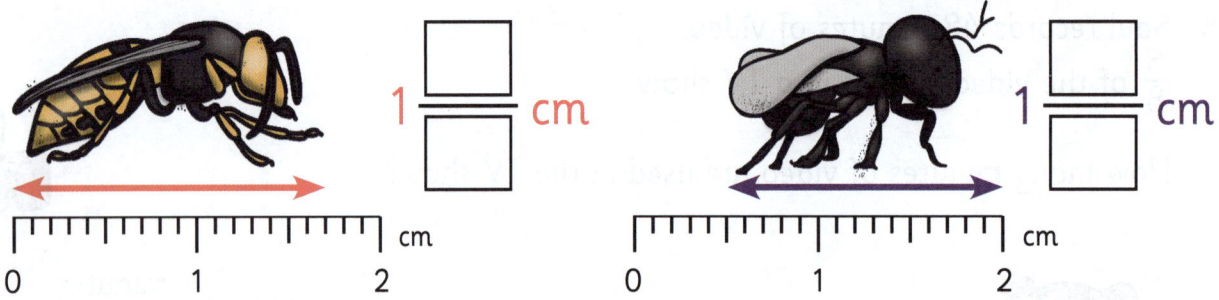

1 ☐/☐ cm   1 ☐/☐ cm

2. Draw lines to match each number sentence to its missing fraction.

$\frac{2}{7} + ? = 1$ $\frac{2}{7} + \frac{4}{7} = ?$ $? + \frac{1}{7} = \frac{5}{7}$

 $\frac{5}{7}$  $\frac{4}{7}$  $\frac{6}{7}$

3. There are 12 leopards in a forest. 7 leopards are asleep.
   What fraction of the leopards are awake?

   ....

4. Shade in more of Shape B so it has the same fraction shaded as Shape A.

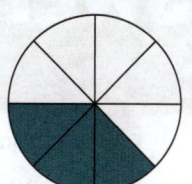 **Shape A**

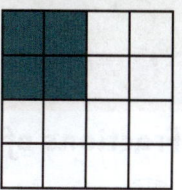 **Shape B**

5. Three chameleons catch some flies.
   Cam catches $\frac{1}{3}$, Mel catches $\frac{1}{2}$ and Leon catches $\frac{1}{6}$ of the flies.

   Write their names in order from most to fewest flies caught.

most ———————————————→ fewest

....

6. Mimi and Milo each think of a number.

   | One quarter of Mimi's number is 3. | | One half of Milo's number is 8. |

   What is the difference between their numbers?

   ....

An Extra Challenge

The pupils in Class 3Y are wearing animal masks. There are 12 girls and 18 boys.

No girls have toucan masks
$\frac{1}{3}$ of boys have toucan masks

2 girls have frog masks
No boys have frog masks

$\frac{2}{3}$ of girls have tiger masks
? of boys have tiger masks

An **equal fraction** of girls and boys have gorilla masks.

Use the tables to help you work out:

a) How many girls have gorilla masks?

b) How many boys have tiger masks?

	Toucan	Frog	Tiger	Gorilla	**Total**
Girls	0				12

	Toucan	Frog	Tiger	Gorilla	**Total**
Boys					18

Do you feel like a tou-can or a tou-can't? Tick a box!

 ☐   ☐  ☐

Answers

Pages 2-3 — Fractions of Shapes

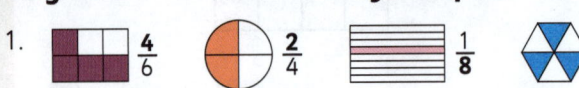

1. $\frac{4}{6}$ $\frac{2}{4}$ $\frac{1}{8}$ $\frac{3}{6}$

2. E.g.

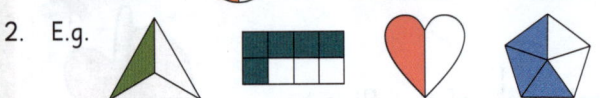

3.

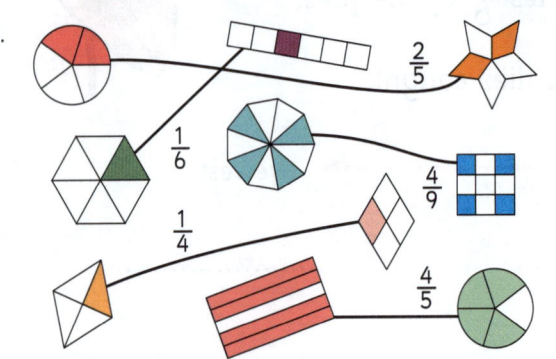

An Extra Challenge

a) **4**th is $\frac{1}{2}$ the size of 3rd.   b) **4**th is $\frac{1}{5}$ the size of 1st.

c) (i) 3rd is $\frac{2}{3}$ the size of 2nd.   (ii) 2nd is $\frac{3}{5}$ the size of 1st.

Pages 4-5 — Tenths

1. three tenths $\frac{4}{10}$ five tenths $\frac{7}{10}$

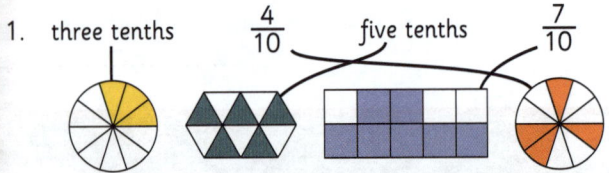

2. There are 10 panels, so: a) $\frac{3}{10}$ b) $\frac{5}{10}$ $\left(\text{or } \frac{1}{2}\right)$

3. a) $\frac{8}{10}$ b) $\frac{2}{10}$ c) more   d) seven

An Extra Challenge

$\frac{7}{10}$ $\frac{5}{10}$ $\frac{9}{10}$ $\frac{8}{10}$

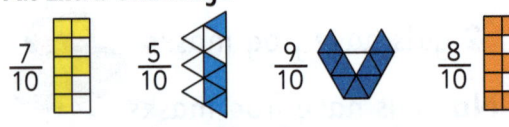

So Beebe's tent number is **five**.

Pages 6-7 — Fractions of Objects

1. a)

   There are 5 bowls in each group, so $\frac{1}{2}$ of 10 = **5**.

   b)

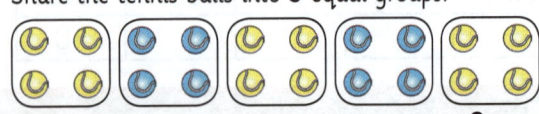

   There are 4 kennels in each group, so $\frac{1}{4}$ of 16 = **4**.

2. Share the tennis balls into 5 equal groups:

   The blue tennis balls make up 2 groups, so $\frac{2}{5}$.

3. Maya has split 18 bones into 3 groups, so the question is "What is $\frac{1}{3}$ of **18**?".

   Each group has 6 bones, so the answer is **6**.

4. Ana has 3 groups of 5, so she takes 5 × 2 = 10 biscuits. Leo has 4 groups of 3, so he takes 3 × 3 = 9 biscuits. So they take 10 + 9 = **19** biscuits in total.

An Extra Challenge

If **2 grey dogs** leave, then 1 grey and 5 brown are left, so $\frac{1}{6}$ are grey.

If **2 brown dogs** leave, then 3 brown and 3 brown are left, so $\frac{3}{6}$ are grey.

If **1 grey dog** and **1 brown dog** leave, then 2 grey and 4 brown are left, so $\frac{2}{6}$ are grey.

So $\frac{1}{6}$, $\frac{3}{6}$ and $\frac{2}{6}$ should be circled.

Pages 8-9 — Equivalent Fractions

1. ✔ ✔ ✔

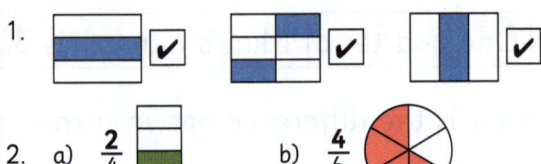

2. a) $\frac{2}{4}$ b) $\frac{4}{6}$

3.  $\frac{3}{5}$ = $\frac{6}{10}$

4.

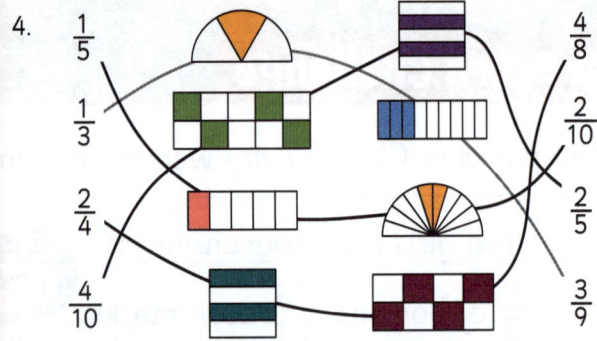

$\frac{1}{5}$ $\frac{4}{8}$

$\frac{1}{3}$ $\frac{2}{10}$

$\frac{2}{4}$ $\frac{2}{5}$

$\frac{4}{10}$ $\frac{3}{9}$

An Extra Challenge

a) 6 out of 12 squares have prints, so $\frac{6}{12}$ $\left(\text{or } \frac{1}{2}\right)$.

b) $\frac{3}{6}$ is an equivalent fraction to $\frac{6}{12}$, so

Pages 10-11 — Adding Fractions

1. $\frac{2}{6}$ + $\frac{3}{6}$ = $\frac{5}{6}$

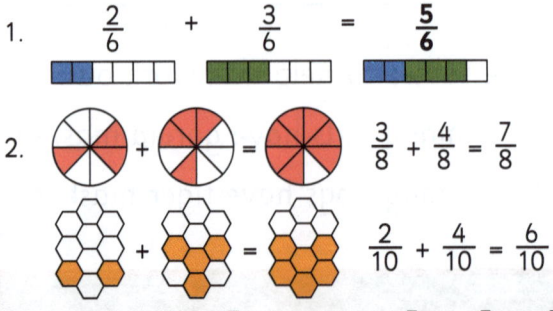

2. $\frac{3}{8}$ + $\frac{4}{8}$ = $\frac{7}{8}$

   $\frac{2}{10}$ + $\frac{4}{10}$ = $\frac{6}{10}$

3. a) $\frac{4}{7}$ + $\frac{1}{7}$ = $\frac{5}{7}$ b) $\frac{5}{13}$ + $\frac{5}{13}$ = $\frac{10}{13}$

4.

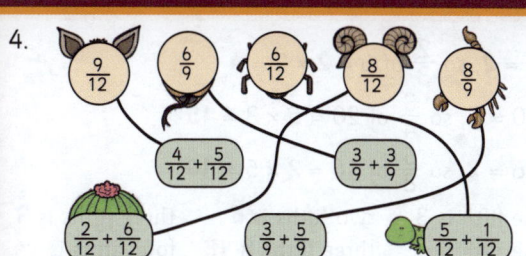

5. a) $\frac{3}{11} + \frac{2}{11} = \mathbf{\frac{5}{11}}$ b) $\frac{3}{11} + \frac{6}{11} = \mathbf{\frac{9}{11}}$

An Extra Challenge

$\frac{2}{5} + \mathbf{\frac{2}{5}} = \frac{4}{5}$ $\frac{5}{8} + \frac{3}{8} = \frac{8}{8}$ $\frac{8}{12} + \frac{3}{12} = \frac{11}{12}$

Pages 12-13 — Subtracting Fractions

1. $\frac{4}{5} - \frac{1}{5} = \mathbf{\frac{3}{5}}$ $\frac{3}{6} - \frac{2}{6} = \mathbf{\frac{1}{6}}$

$\frac{6}{9} - \frac{2}{9} = \mathbf{\frac{4}{9}}$ $\frac{8}{9} - \frac{6}{9} = \mathbf{\frac{2}{9}}$

2. $\frac{5}{8} - \frac{2}{8} = \mathbf{\frac{3}{8}}$

3. $\frac{11}{12} - \mathbf{\frac{6}{12}} = \frac{5}{12}$ $\frac{9}{12} - \frac{7}{12} = \frac{2}{12}$

$\mathbf{\frac{8}{12}} - \frac{5}{12} = \frac{3}{12}$

4. 1 (whole) $= \frac{10}{10}$

The bookshelf starts with $\frac{10}{10}$ of the books, so

there are $\frac{10}{10} - \frac{3}{10} = \mathbf{\frac{7}{10}}$ of the books left.

An Extra Challenge

The fractions that Oli and Caleb subtract must make a total difference of $\frac{10}{11} - \frac{4}{11} = \frac{6}{11}$. For example, Oli could subtract $\frac{5}{11}$ and Caleb could subtract $\frac{1}{11}$.

You also could have found these pairs (in either order):

$\frac{5}{11}$ and $\frac{1}{11}$ $\frac{4}{11}$ and $\frac{2}{11}$ $\frac{3}{11}$ and $\frac{3}{11}$

Pages 14-15 — High Street Jumble

Florist: **E**

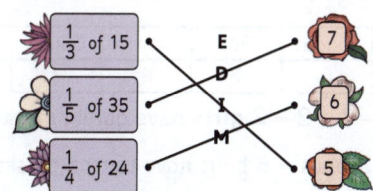

Grocers: **N** $\left(\frac{2}{8} + \frac{3}{8} = \frac{5}{8}\right)$

Newsagents: From largest to smallest, the fractions are: $\frac{1}{7}$, $\mathbf{\frac{1}{9}}$, $\frac{1}{10}$, $\frac{1}{13}$, $\frac{1}{18}$. So her letter is **S**.

Bakery: **B** $\left(\frac{11}{12} - \frac{4}{12} = \frac{7}{12}\right)$

Boutique: $\frac{1}{5}$ of 20 = 20 ÷ 5 = 4, so $\frac{3}{5}$ of 20 = 4 × 3 = 12

12 + 2 = 14, so her letter is **A**.

So her letters are E, N, S, B and A. The word is **BEANS**.

Pages 16-17 — Ordering Fractions 1

1. a) $\frac{4}{5}$ b) $\frac{6}{8}$

2.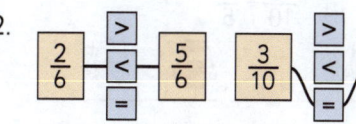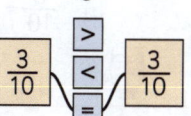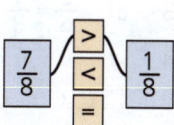

3. 6 is the largest numerator, so $\frac{6}{12}$ is the largest.

So **Helen** collects the most rocks.

4. From smallest to largest: $\frac{2}{7}$, $\frac{3}{7}$, $\frac{5}{7}$, $\frac{6}{7}$

5. From largest to smallest, the fractions are: $\frac{5}{9}$, $\frac{3}{9}$, $\frac{1}{9}$

So the order of the names is: Val, Ebop, Sram

An Extra Challenge

From largest to smallest, the fractions for cooking are:

$\frac{5}{11}$ (Matt), $\frac{3}{11}$ (Mae), $\frac{2}{11}$ (Lizzy), $\frac{1}{11}$ (Peter)

From largest to smallest, the fractions for cleaning are:

$\frac{6}{14}$ (Lizzy), $\frac{4}{14}$ (Peter), $\frac{3}{14}$ (Mae), $\frac{1}{14}$ (Matt)

So Matt has 4 + 1 = **5** points, Mae has 3 + 2 = **5**, Lizzy has 2 + 4 = **6** and Peter has 1 + 3 = **4**.

Pages 18-19 — Ordering Fractions 2

1. $\frac{1}{2} > \frac{1}{3}$ $\frac{1}{7} < \frac{1}{5}$ $\frac{1}{10} < \frac{1}{4}$

2. Anne's car: Maisie, Keaton, Liu
Tony's car: Jos, Lily, Benoit

3.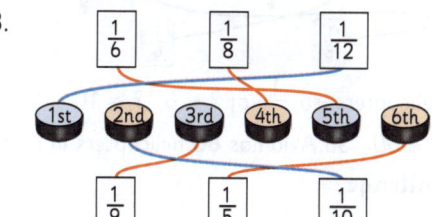

4. From largest to smallest: $\frac{1}{4}$, $\frac{1}{6}$, $\frac{1}{7}$, $\frac{1}{11}$

So the order of the colours is: white, red, blue, orange.

An Extra Challenge

From largest to smallest, the fractions are:

$\frac{1}{2}$, $\frac{1}{4}$, $\frac{1}{7}$, Maisie's, $\frac{1}{28}$. The denominator of

Maisie's fraction is between 7 and 28, so it must be **14**.

Answers

Pages 20-21 — On the Number Line

1.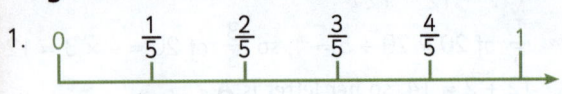

2.

3. a) $\frac{2}{6} = \frac{1}{3}$ b) $\frac{8}{10} = \frac{4}{5}$

4.

5. Count up in quarters from 5 — the number is $5\frac{3}{4}$.

   An Extra Challenge

   The owls at $2\frac{4}{6}$ and $3\frac{2}{9}$ are in the correct place.
   The correct number line is:

   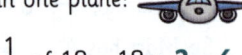

Pages 22-23 — Fractions of Amounts 1

1. $\frac{1}{5}$ of 5 = 5 ÷ 5 = **1**, so colour in one plane:

2. $\frac{1}{10}$ of 20 = 20 ÷ **10** = **2** $\frac{1}{3}$ of 18 = 18 ÷ **3** = **6**

3.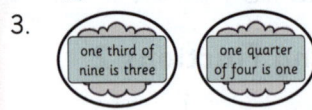

   one third of nine is three   one quarter of four is one

4. $\frac{1}{8}$ of 32 = 32 ÷ 8 = **4** hot air balloons

5.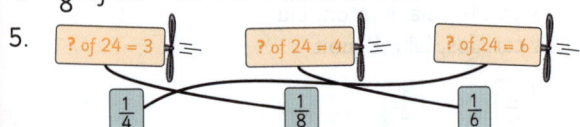

6. There are 6 helicopters, so $\frac{1}{10}$ of ? = 6. ? ÷ 10 = 6,
   so ? = 10 × 6 = 60. So Akio has **60** helicopters in total.

   An Extra Challenge

   $\frac{1}{4}$ of 12 = 3, so **3** bags are black.
   This leaves 12 − 3 = 9 bags. $\frac{1}{9}$ of 9 = 1,
   so 1 bag is red. This leaves 9 − 1 = 8 bags.
   $\frac{1}{2}$ of 8 = 4, so **4 bags** are brown.

Pages 24-25 — Fractions of Amounts 2

1. a) $\frac{1}{4}$ of 8 = **2**, $\frac{3}{4}$ of 8 = **6**

   b) $\frac{1}{5}$ of 10 = **2**, $\frac{3}{5}$ of 10 = **6**

2. $\frac{1}{3}$ of 6 = **2**, so $\frac{2}{3}$ of 6 = 2 × 2 = **4**
   $\frac{1}{4}$ of 20 = **5**, so $\frac{3}{4}$ of 20 = 5 × 3 = **15**
   $\frac{1}{8}$ of 16 = **2**, so $\frac{5}{8}$ of 16 = 2 × 5 = **10**

3. 15: one fifth is 3   two fifths is **6**   three fifths is **9**
   30: one fifth is **6**   three fifths is **18**   four fifths is **24**

4. $\frac{1}{10}$ of £40 = £40 ÷ 10 = £4, so
   $\frac{7}{10}$ of £40 = £4 × 7 = **£28**

5. $\frac{1}{8}$ of 48 = 48 ÷ 8 = 6, so $\frac{5}{8}$ of 48 = 6 × 5 = **30** mins

   An Extra Challenge

   a) $\frac{1}{4}$ of £80 = £20, so $\frac{3}{4}$ of £80 = £20 × 3 = **£60**

   b) $\frac{1}{3}$ of 60 = 20, so $\frac{2}{3}$ of 60 = 20 × 2 = **40** sheep

   c) If $\frac{2}{4}$ of ? = 8, then $\frac{1}{4}$ of ? = 4. ? ÷ 4 = 4, so
      ? = 4 × 4 = 16. So Moon City have played **16** games.

Pages 26-27 — Fraction Problems

1. $1\frac{7}{10}$ cm $1\frac{5}{10}$ cm (or $1\frac{1}{2}$ cm)

2.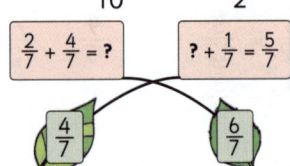

3. 12 − 7 = 5, so $\frac{5}{12}$ of the leopards are awake.

4. Shape A: $\frac{3}{8}$ shaded   Shape B: $\frac{4}{16}$ shaded
   $\frac{3}{8} = \frac{6}{16}$, so shade **2 more squares** of Shape B.

5. From most to fewest: Mel, Cam, Leon

6. $\frac{1}{4}$ of ? = 3. ? ÷ 4 = 3, so ? = 4 × 3 = 12. So Mimi's
   number is 12. $\frac{1}{2}$ of ? = 8. ? ÷ 2 = 8, so ? = 2 × 8 = 16.
   So Milo's number is 16. The difference is 16 − 12 = **4**.

   An Extra Challenge

   a) $\frac{1}{3}$ of 12 girls = 12 ÷ 3 = 4, so
      $\frac{2}{3}$ of 12 girls = 4 × 2 = 8 girls have tiger masks.

	Toucan	Frog	Tiger	Gorilla	Total
Girls	0	2	8	?	12

   So 12 − 8 − 2 = **2 girls** have gorilla masks.

   b) $\frac{1}{3}$ of 18 boys = 6 boys have toucan masks.
      $\frac{2}{12} = \frac{1}{6}$ of girls have gorilla masks, so
      $\frac{1}{6}$ of 18 boys = 3 boys have gorilla masks.

	Toucan	Frog	Tiger	Gorilla	Total
Boys	6	0	?	3	18

   So 18 − 6 − 3 = **9 boys** have tiger masks.

MPFF3Q21